P9-DHS-331

3 1257 01385 1307

Schaumburg Township District Library

130 South Roselle Road

Schaumburg, Illinois 60193

**Schaumburg Township
District Library**
schaumburglibrary.org
Renewals: (847) 923-3158

Maple Trees

By Allan Fowler

Consultants
Martha Walsh, Reading Specialist

Jan Jenner, Ph.D.

SCHAUMBURG TOWNSHIP DISTRICT LIBRARY
JUVENILE DEPT
130 SOUTH ROSELLE ROAD
SCHAUMBURG, ILLINOIS 60193

ℚℙ Children's Press®
A Division of Scholastic Inc.
New York   Toronto   London   Auckland   Sydney
Mexico City   New Delhi   Hong Kong
Danbury, Connecticut

EASY
583.78
FOW

3 1257 01385 1307

Designer: Herman Adler Design
Photo Researcher: Caroline Anderson
The photo on the cover shows a maple tree covered by colorful
autumn leaves.

Library of Congress Cataloging-in-Publication Data

Fowler, Allan.
    Maple trees / by Allan Fowler.
      p. cm. — (Rookie read-about science)
    Summary: This introductory book discusses leaves, sap, and the different
kinds of maple trees.
    ISBN 0-516-21684-8 (lib. bdg.)   0-516-25985-7 (pbk.)
    1. Maple—Juvenile literature. [1. Maple. 2. Trees.] I. Title. II. Series.
QK495.A17 F68   2001
583'.78—dc21

                         00-055508

©2001 Children's Press®
A Division of Scholastic Inc.
All rights reserved. Published simultaneously in Canada.
Printed in the United States of America.
1 2 3 4 5 6 7 8 9 10 R 10 09 08 07 06 05 04 03 02 01

Have you ever eaten
pancakes dripping
with maple syrup?

4

Sweet maple syrup comes from maple trees.

Maple trees grow in the northeastern United States and eastern Canada.

You can recognize most maple trees by their leaves.

A maple leaf has three parts. These parts are called lobes.

Each lobe comes to a point.

lobe

Maple leaves grow in pairs on branches. One leaf grows on each side of the branch.

Big, leafy maple trees give us shade from the hot sun. They are often planted in yards and parks and along streets.

Some streets are named
after the maple trees that
grow there.

Small flowers grow on maple trees. Seeds from the flowers have wings.

The wings help them float in the wind. If the seeds land in good soil, they can grow into new trees.

There are different kinds of maple trees. Syrup comes from sugar maples.

People tap these trees in early spring. They drill holes in the trees.

Then they put spouts, or
small pipes, into the holes.

The sap, or juice, of the
maple tree comes out of
the spouts. It drips into
buckets. This does not
hurt the tree.

People take the buckets
of sap to a sugarhouse.

They boil the sap into
syrup at the sugarhouse.

Most maple syrup comes from Quebec, Canada.

There is even a maple leaf
on the Canadian flag.

Sugar maples give us more than just syrup.

Their wood is very hard. So maple trees are used to make things, such as furniture and musical instruments.

Maple trees change color in the fall. Green maple leaves turn yellow, orange, red, or gold.

Then the maple trees lose their leaves. The trees stay bare until spring.

Many people rake the colorful maple leaves into piles. Then kids have fun jumping into them!

Words You Know

Canadian flag

flowers

leaves

lobes

sap

seeds

shade

sugarhouse

syrup

Index

branches, 8, 9

Canada, 5, 22

Canadian flag, 22, 23

fall, 26

flowers, 12

furniture, 25

holes, 16, 17

leaves, 6, 8, 9, 26, 27, 28, 29

lobes, 6, 7

musical instruments, 24, 25

pancakes, 3

parks, 10

sap, 18, 19, 20, 21

seeds, 12

shade, 10

soil, 13

spouts, 17, 19

spring, 16, 26

streets, 10, 11

sugarhouse, 20, 21

syrup, 3, 5, 14, 21, 22, 25

United States, 5

wings, 12, 13

yards, 10

About the Author

Allan Fowler is a freelance writer with a background in advertising. Born in New York, he now lives in Chicago and enjoys traveling.

Photo Credits

Photographs ©: Dembinsky Photo Assoc.: 11 (Adam Jones), 10, 31 center left (Richard Hamilton Smith); Envision/Rudy Muller: 3, 31 bottom; Photo Researchers, NY: 18, 31 top left (John Bova), 12, 30 top right (Geoff Bryant), 13, 31 top right (R. J. Erwin), 27 (Adam Jones), 7, 30 bottom right (John Kaprielian), 8, 30 bottom left (Pat Lynch), 13 inset (Rod Planck), cover (Ah Rider); PhotoEdit/Jeff Greenberg: 24; Stone/Donna Day: 28; The Image Works: 16, 17, 21, 31 center right (M. Granitsas), 22 (Michael Greeniar), 20 (Alden Pellett); Visuals Unlimited: 23, 30 top left (Arthur Morris), 15 (Glenn Oliver), 4 (Doug Sokell).